Encore! Encore!

Seniors (50 plus) as Entrepreneurs:
Their Time Has Come

By: Joe Wasylyk

Founder of
"The Seniorpreneur Project"

Special Thanks

Joe

Special thanks to Warren Semotiuk of **DragonWorx Productions** (www.DragonWorxLair.com) for collaborative, editorial, and computer consulting services work.

Warren

Very special thanx and love to my son, Tyler Semotiuk, for being a light that never goes out.

Special thanx to the best pizza place in Edmonton, **Pizzera Prego** (www.pregopizza.com) for being a very gracious marathon business meeting host.

Thanx to **Bistro 112** – the coolest internet café in Edmonton and the best place to work on writing, editing, and general computer stuff.

Thanx to Joe for giving me the opportunity of a lifetime to help actualize your vision. We met the challenges and now the dream is a reality!

TABLE OF CONTENTS

Chapter 1   Successful Senior Entrepreneurs

Chapter 2   Retirement Lifestyle

Chapter 3   Dare to Dream

Chapter 4   Do I Need a Business Plan?

Chapter 5   Dreaming Big, Starting Small

Chapter 6   Caution – Exhaustion Ahead?

Chapter 7   Public Policy and Aging

Chapter 8   Maturity, Wisdom, and Confidence

Chapter 9   Philanthropy and Building a Legacy

Chapter 10 Career Transition – More Help

DEDICATION

Dedicated to the memory of my brother George Wasylyk who passed away at the age of 59 on December 12, 2005. Although he died too early, with the dream still in him, he had a very creative spirit. He would have been a natural participant in the new age of the Seniorpreneur.

Also, an honorable mention to my children Michael and Carrie-Ann and to grandchildren Caitlin, Teija, and Rebekah.

INTRODUCTION

Many seniors have elected to become first-time entrepreneurs after age sixty. Economic factors and a job market perceived to be biased against older workers has pushed a number of people into starting his or her own business.

Sara Rix, a strategic advisor of AARP (American Association of Retired Persons), says that in a recent survey in which people were asked what they expected to do when they retire, 15% responded that they were going to go into business for themselves.

"Unemployment rates are lower for the older population," she says. "But they are increasing for those 55 and up. And it's been dramatic since the recession began."

Rix notes that when older people are laid off, they remain unemployed longer than younger counterparts. They are also subjected to a number of barriers such as the perception that they lack marketable skills.

"In that case," says Rix, "starting a business may seem the only feasible alternative in a down economy even though they may not have an easy go of starting a business."

Very little is known about the entrepreneurial potential of individuals in the Third Age (50 – 75 years old).

Most research is devoted to understanding and promoting entrepreneurship in younger age groups. Recent progress has been made for other demographic groups such as aboriginal or immigrant but empirical research is practically non-existent for the seniors (50 plus) demographic group. There are also substantial gaps in understanding the attitudes of the over 50's to self-employment.

PRIME has published an interim report called "Olderpreneur Outcomes". The good news is that 43% have gone ahead and started a business, 30% were still considering it, and only 27% had given up. Most of these people were in their 50's.

Furthermore, only 15% of the respondents were people in their 60's or 70's. This is reflected in the business outcomes, with most (84%) of the people starting a business being in their 50's as well.

As a result, we are going to need new strategies in order to accomplish the goal of having more seniors in their 60's, 70's, and 80's start his or her own business.

A recent study on older entrepreneurship (Curran and Blackburn, 2001) indicated that younger individuals exhibit higher productivity and energy than older counterparts.

This suggests that while the ability to establish or run a business is higher at an older age, the motivation or desire for entrepreneurial behavior is significantly lower.

This is keeping with the more general conclusions from a recent Norwegian study of entrepreneurs over the age of 18, which found that while entrepreneurial competencies increase with age, entrepreneurial intentions tend to decrease (Rotefoss and Kolvereid, 2005).

Similar to the findings of Curran and Blackburn, interest in starting a business or motivation seems to drop off more rapidly for women than men, with the PRIME report suggesting that very few women in their 60's and 70's actually start or run a business.

A current local newspaper headline reads: "Ponzi Frauds a Growth Industry in Tough Times". Why are normally prudent people falling victim to so-called surefire investment opportunities at high profits? They have visions of big dollar signs in their heads -- the unbelievable Return on Investment (ROI) of 20% or much more.

Financial advisors and others have often asked clients to maximize RRSP or 401K plans to have a source of savings for retirement. Most people are often initially skeptical about any investments being promoted in a business seminar setting, still many of these same people signed up anyway -- they de-register some of their own RRSPs or 401K plans and don't hesitate to pluck down anywhere between $10,000 and $100,000 on a risky investment.

What is really happening here?

It seems like people are losing control regarding their own financial well being. I wrote this book to sound the alarm and find a business model that could help seniors regain control of their hard-earned financial resources -- leading to a creative, productive, and prosperous retirement life.

MISSION STATEMENT

On November 9, 2006 I started the 'Seniorpreneur Project' on the web site called www.seniorsdaily.net. On this website I posted my first message -- a mustard seed that grew into a movement:

"I would like to take the subjects of finances and lifestyle for seniors to a different higher level. Hopefully, this could see a movement where seniors are empowered to become entrepreneurs, or as I understand them to be seniorpreneurs. This would enable seniors to live a more enlightened retirement life and give them a great option to be more productive and be able to contribute more to society."

Can seniors benefit or be successful in starting a business? Will seniors share a 'Crown of Life' with the rest of society or instead settle for a subsistence lifestyle producing minimum results and satisfaction towards the end of life?

The encore stage is now set for the emerging baby boomer to have and enjoy a for-profit entrepreneurial or a non-profit encore career.

Boomers are defined as people born between 1946 and 1964 – a vast number just reaching retirement age.

I was born on May 21, 1945 in Edmonton, Alberta. I have a Business Education degree from the University of Alberta. I also have a Purchasing Management and Research background both in private industry and the public service with the Government of Alberta.

I owned my own corporate company in the fields of Purchasing Services, Food Equipment Sales, and Tax Accounting for Small Business. I have also helped the aboriginal demographic group in the province of Alberta with business development consulting services.

In a research paper titled "Understanding the Grey Entrepreneur" by Paul Weber and Michael Schaper (2004) the opening sentence reads:

"Demographic trends in the developed world indicate that older entrepreneurs will play an increasingly important part of economic activity as populations age yet this cohort has been largely ignored in entrepreneurship research."

My research indicates that a majority of older entrepreneurs are male, although the number of older female entrepreneurs is increasing. They are less likely to possess formal education than younger entrepreneurs.

The disadvantages or potential barriers faced by older entrepreneurs can include lower levels of health, energy, and productivity, ageism, and the value that his or her society places on active "productive" aging.

The advantages that older entrepreneurs possess include **greater levels of technical and management experience**, superior personal networks, and a stronger financial asset base.

What are the differences between younger and older entrepreneurs?

What are the motives and success criteria?

What is the impact of financial knowledge on venturing behavior?

What is the role of government policies in fostering individual enterprise?

What is the significance of cultural differences amongst older entrepreneurs?

Business Week (June 8, 2009) stated:

"While many have elected to become first-time entrepreneurs after 60, a number of economic factors and a job market perceived to be biased against older workers have pushed a number of people into starting their own businesses."

With so many retirees finding pensions and retirement savings dented and a rising unemployment rate -- now averaging around 10% in the USA and 8% in Canada -- the trend toward aged entrepreneurs is poised to grow.

Dr. Suresh Patel and Professor Colin Gray of the United Kingdom Business School attempted to analyze the following question:

"What predisposes 'Grey Entrepreneurs' to increasing entrepreneurial activity?"

There is an interplay of push and pull factors (Bururu, 1998; Clark and Drinkwater, 1998; McGregor and Tweed, 1998) that explain the trend of the Grey community into self-employment and enterprise:

The push factors include:
- disadvantage in the labor market
- redundancy
- not able to find work again
- age discrimination
- decline in traditional corporate career opportunities
- insufficient retirement funds
- inadequacy of existing pension arrangement and entitlements

The **pull** factors include:
- business opportunities
- independence
- portfolio careers
- growth in knowledge service economy
- increasing recognition of home-based businesses

The need for income itself is probably the greatest single motive for self-employment. Interest in the work itself can also be a key motivation for starting a business. A chance to apply long-honed skills and long-practiced hobbies is a strong driver -- especially when coupled with the alternative prospect of unemployment.

For many older workers, neither energy nor financial considerations are greater obstacles than that of younger persons. Self-employment is mainly motivated either by a desire for independence of action based on the assets of experience or as a last resort out of economic need against a background of discrimination.

Arkebauer, J.B. (1995), "Golden Entrepreneuring: The Mature Person's Guide to a Successful Business", has coined the phrase 'Seniorpreneur' to denote any individual over the age of 50 who owns a business -- regardless of size.

ARE YOU A SENIORPRENEUR IN THE MAKING?

In the book, "How to Make the Rest of Your Life the Best of Your Life", Mark Victor Hansen and Art Linkletter said:

"If you possess three important characteristics – physical readiness, the capacity to enjoy risks, and a passion for learning new things – then becoming a seniorpreneur could be the most rewarding aspect of your later life."

This is your chance to think creatively.
- What assets do you bring to the table?
- How could you take what you're BEST at and make a career of it?
- What retirement lifestyle do you want in your retirement?

Chapter 1
Successful Senior Entrepreneurs

"The rules of money changed in 1971. Today, we see the tragic results of that change. The tragedy shows up in the lives of people who are not only out of work, but in many instances too old to go back to work. The tragedy is the erosion of their savings as inflation marches on."

- Robert Kiyosaki

Can seniors be successful in starting a business?

NEVER TOO OLD

"What becomes fragile when we age is not our bodies as much as our egos. The best time to take some daring steps is when we get older."

- Helen Hayes

People who passed their sixtieth birthday have made many of the world's greatest accomplishments.

Those people, some better known than others, show that there are certainly no present age limits for achievement.

- At age eighty, owner and former publisher of the Washington Post, Katherine Graham, won a Pulitzer Prize for her bestselling autobiography – her first and only book.

- John Glenn, the first man to orbit the Earth in the early 1960s, trained for another space launch more than thirty years later. During his training, the seventy-plus Glenn joined the rest of the space crew in challenging physical practice exercises. America's oldest astronaut blasted towards the heavens once again – this time to learn about aging in space.

- Billy Graham, in his early eighties, continues to be one of the most influential men in the world. He is said to have preached to greater multitudes than anyone else alive. In keeping with the times, he recently opened a home page on

the internet.
- History also shows that some of the greatest world leaders continued to work for progress into his or her later years. Winston Churchill did not become Prime Minister of England until he was sixty-two, after a lifetime of defeats and setbacks. His greatest victories and contributions came when he was a senior citizen.

- Jimmy Carter, the thirty-ninth President, became a distinguished professor at Emory University and founded the Carter Center at the age of fifty-eight. At age sixty-seven, he launched the Atlanta Project, a community-wide effort to attack the social problems associated with poverty. Today he actively works on the behalf of the "Habitat for Humanity" programs -- dedicated to providing low-income families new homes built by volunteers.

- Many firsts have been accomplished by people sixty and over. George Eastman, founder of the Eastman Kodak Company, was raised in poverty. He appreciated money for what it could do. He cared little for holding it for himself. At the age of sixty-five, he gave one-third of his own holdings of company stock -- worth ten million dollars -- to his employees. He was among the first industrialists to establish fringe benefits to his employees.

- People have often established enduring organizations and causes over the age of sixty. At the age of sixty-five, Dr. Ethel Percy Andrus founded and became president of the National Retired Teachers Association, and at the age of seventy-four she founded the American Association of Retired Persons.

- After that, she added a pharmacy service, a travel service (first in the country), the institute of Lifetime Learning and the AARP International to her list of accomplishments.

- Are you merely growing older, or like many of these shining examples, are you continuing to be active and useful as the

years go by? It IS possible.
- As Jane Brody, health writer of the New York Times, puts it: "To die young, as late in life as possible.

  - Jack Canfield, Mark Victor Hansen, Paul J. Meyer, and Amy Seeger

It's possible!

Why did I want to write this book?

I wanted to study and research the answers to these seemingly unanswerable questions.

Can seniors (50 plus) benefit from starting a business?

- Is it possible for a sixty or sixty-five year old man or woman living only on social security pensions to empower themselves and have a more creative and satisfying retirement life?

- Is it possible to change the traditional late-life model of withdrawal and entitlement into a new paradigm?

- Why is an aging society seen solely in terms of increasing dependency and as primarily being a consumer? Why do we rarely see seniors as active and creative producers or seniorpreneurs?

- When will society see aging as a lifelong learning opportunitity – a great way to become better equipped to fight feelings of boredom, despair, and loss of usefulness?

Stage of Life Perception

A possible problem to consider here is that self-image status feeds fears about life after work. Most people associate retiring with the final stage of life. They also question what it will mean to their overall health. They associate this stage of life with a deterioration of the body. It's a perception, rather than reality.

Are there things you want to pursue that you haven't yet? You need to expand your definition of who you are. Your own unique life circumstances can be the **key to finding something** that you want to work on in the final stages of life.

How do you function best? How are you wired and in what circumstances do you work best? What natural talents and learned skills do you have to contribute? For example, Colonel Harland Sanders of KFC had cooking skills.

Do you have any hidden gifts that may yet to be discovered?

Focus on your natural talents, favorite skills, and knowledge you have gained over the years.

Is there any product or service that you can demonstrate to have above average sales potential? An example would be Colonel Sanders and his secret chicken-seasoning recipe.

What excites you?

What are you passionate about?

Why are you on the planet? Take as an article of faith that you were put on this Earth for a purpose. You have been given the gifts you will need to achieve your mission.

Because of a lifetime of preparation, Colonel Sanders only took about one year to decide what he was going to do after he reached sixty-five years old. You may take two to five years or more to shake off old habits -- discovering your heartfelt passions and creating new pathways.

Take an incredible journey of self-discovery to uncover the many needs in our world today and how you can help meet those needs.

Encore careers are a fantastic option – finding solutions to social issues in the areas of health care, education, environment, and poverty issues in our communities.

Business Initiative and Inspiration

My main inspiration for writing this book has come from studying the life of Colonel Harland Sanders. In 1974, Colonel Sanders had 50,000 copies of his book published -- "Life as I Have Known It Has Been 'Finger Lickin' Good'" (Creation House, Illinois 60187).

I personally own two copies of this book.

Colonel Sanders, Robert Kiyosaki, and Art Linkletter conquered defeat and retirement boredom by continuing to be active and productive after age sixty-five.

This book was written to show that seniors are part of a lifelong learning process and are able to choose to be a seniorpreneur -- rather than withdraw and only pursue leisure type of activities.

Throughout his life Colonel Sanders faced many challenges in both his personal and business life. When the Colonel turned sixty-five years old he had only a Social Security cheque in the amount of $105 US to live on, with the addition of some savings from auctioning off his motel and restaurant.

He received in the amount of $75,000 US dollars. Unfortunately, most of this amount was used to pay taxes and other outstanding bills.

The present economic meltdown regarding the state of the stock market and real estate property investments is the dilemma that a lot of seniors find themselves in today. What are you going to do to increase your retirement savings? What did Colonel Sanders do in his rather desperate situation?

Are you going to feel hopeless and say to yourself that your life is over?

Will you sit in a rocking chair and make a fuss over meager government pensions?

Think about your own encore career and start pursuing business ideas that you can develop yourself.

This will enable you to become more creative, productive, and prosperous in your retirement life.

RICH SENIOR

A positive and very creative person, Colonel Sanders turned a setback in victory.

Harland was born on September 8, 1890 into a very large, very poor family. His father labored in the Kentucky coal mines to support a family of seven, but died when Harland was just six years old. His mother took a job in a garment factory, which left the task of caring for his siblings – including doing much of the cooking – to Harland, the oldest of the five children.

When his mother remarried, Harland and his stepfather didn't see eye-to-eye, so he hit the road – at the ripe age of twelve. The next twenty-five years of his life was a work in progress; he failed at more jobs during that period than most people will ever try. With little guidance and less formal education, he was making life up as he went along.

He worked as a farm hand, a streetcar conductor, a private in the U.S. Army in Cuba, a blacksmith's apprentice, a rail-yard fireman for Southern Railway, a ferryboat captain, an insurance salesman, a tire salesman, and a service station manager for Standard Oil.

He also studied law by correspondence, and in the midst of his vocational success, he married at eighteen and had a child.

But then he began discovering natural talents. In 1930, in the middle of the Great Depression, in a service station he managed in Kentucky, he started preparing and serving meals. He pumped gas, cooked food, and ran the cash register – the epitome of the proverbial "chief cook and bottle washer".

But it worked! Maybe it was his early training at the stove as a child cooking for his siblings. Whatever it was, people liked his food – especially his fried chicken.

They liked it so much the word spread and he actually began to make money. He expanded

Sanders Court and Café to include a motel and a restaurant seating 142 people. In 1936 the Governor of the state awarded him the honorary rank of "Kentucky Colonel" in recognition of his contribution to the state's cuisine.

The entire place burned down in 1938, but Colonel Sanders rebuilt it and pressed forward. **That year was momentous for more than the fire.**

When Colonel Sanders attended a demonstration of a new kitchen device called a pressure cooker, he wondered if he could use it to speed up the process of preparing chicken.

When he put in his chicken, coated with his secret recipe of eleven herbs and spices in the pressure cooker, it was a "Eureka!" moment. In 1940, his "original recipe" chicken was born.

Colonel Sanders began traveling the country demonstrating his pressure-cooked, secret spiced chicken to restaurant owners. For the princely sum of five cents for every chicken they cooked, he would teach them his pressure cooker technique and furnish them with his secret spice recipe.

The franchise idea was born.

In 1952, Interstate 75 was built through Eastern Kentucky -- bypassing the small town of Corbin.

The Colonel's motel and restaurant traffic disappeared within months of the freeway opening, and he was forced to sell everything.

After settling his bills, Colonel Sanders was penniless at the age of sixty-five.

SOCIAL SECURITY SURVIVAL

Then, as Harland Sanders sat on his front porch, the mailman came up the steps and handed him an envelope.

It was from the US Government and contained his first Social Security cheque in the amount of $105. At first he stared at the cheque. This man was a Child of God and there was something surging within that said, "My life isn't over and I'm not going to sit in a rocking chair and take money from the government".

So, he began to pray -- and to think. He thought about franchising restaurants that would feature his mother's fried chicken. With his second wife Claudia mixing and bagging spices at home, he hit the road again with his pressure cooker.

He worked hard to convince others to invest in the idea. Kentucky Fried Chicken became an almost instant success. Within five years there were four hundred restaurants selling Kentucky Fried Chicken, and six hundred by 1964.

The Colonel built up a spectacular business and when he retired at 80 years of age, he became a living, walking emissary of the company. Money didn't interest him. He gave it away as fast as he made it.

Chapter 2
How much can I afford to risk?

"If you possess three important characteristics – physical readiness, the capacity to enjoy risks, and have a passion for learning new things – then becoming a seniorpreneur could be the most rewarding aspect of your later life.

This is your chance to think creatively. What assets do you bring to the table? How could you take what your best at and make a new (Encore) career out of it – on your own terms?"

- Art Linkletter and Mark Victor Hansen

"How to Make the Rest of Your Life the Best of Your Life."

DIGNIFIED RETIREMENT

The older baby boomers are in a financial dilemma.

Will they finally achieve social and political power? Will they take on the persona of being unimportant, invisible, politically weak, socially discountable, and economically insignificant?

David Bank, Editor of Encore.org summarized these concerns by saying that, "This year's huge federal deficit makes the staggering long-term shortfall in Social Security and Medicare impossible to ignore any longer."

In response to President Obama's call for "a new era of responsibility", David wants baby boomers to extend their working lives with encore careers in order to realize a win-win-win situation of responsibility, retirement security, and social renewal.

The more costly alternative to provide a dignified retirement for seniors will be to increase Social Security payments. The more effective solution is to create new ways to contribute to society with entrepreneurial projects or with encore careers.

BANKRUPTCY RISING

"In past generations, older Americans were more financially secure," says Elizabeth Warren, a Harvard Law professor and co-author of the Consumer Bankruptcy Project study. "Now instead of going into retirement loaded with assets, Americans are hitting their retirement years loaded with debt."

In previous decades, Social Security helped lift millions of older Americans into a solidly middle class life. With the rising cost of food, drugs, and housing, Social Security often doesn't go far enough.

As a result, many seniors are dropping into the lower class having to take to the streets for a better standard of living.

For the elderly, bankruptcy is a particular concern because it's typically harder for seniors to climb back out of it.

"They have so little time to start over and build up savings, and they have few or no job opportunities," says Susan Reinhard, director of the AARP Public Policy Institute.

"The connection between health and economic security is a big issue for older Americans."

From 1991 to 2007, the rate of personal bankruptcy filings among those aged 65 or older jumped by 150% according to AARP, which will release the new research from Consumer Bankruptcy Project.

The most startling rise occurred among those aged 75 to 84, whose rate soared 433%.

USA President Obama mentioned in his inaugural speech the goal of a 'dignified retirement' for seniors. Elderly North Americans have been seeking bankruptcy court protection at sharply faster rates than other adults.

What solutions do we need to help seniors swamped by debt and rising medical bills?

ENCORE CAREERS

While baby boomers fret about delaying retirement, observers say they still have a chance to rebound by working on entrepreneurial projects and encore careers.

It is the members of the "silent generation" – three million members in Canada born between 1925 and 1945 – who may face the collapse without time to rebuild.

The richest in this group could probably participate more in encore careers to have an opportunity to give back to society.

The poorest in this group born between 1925 and 1945 will need access to affordable housing to alleviate some of these pressures caused by the economic downtrend.

The worst-case scenario is that poorer pensioners will drop behind in real terms and face increasing poverty – aided only by government handouts.

GUARANTEED ANNUAL INCOME

Poverty among older Canadians is exacerbated by the lack of savings by Canadian workers before they retire. Some 35% of Canadian 65-plus currently receive a Guaranteed Income Supplement (GIS) benefit.

The GIS program ensures a minimum annual income of only $13,683 -- the sum of the GIS and Old Age Security (GAS) maximum benefit rates as of September 2008.

This is lower than the poverty level income measured by the low-income cut-off of $15,336 for 2008.

If pensioners cannot participate in a seniorpreneur project or an encore career, then the federal government could provide a guaranteed annual income that is reasonably above the calculated poverty level income.

This would be another option to provide a dignified retirement for all seniors.

SENIOR POVERTY

The conference board of Canada reports that poverty rates among Canadian seniors doubled between 1995 and 2005.

One-third of Canadian workers aged 24 to 64 have no personal retirement savings at all, and 61.5 per cent of workers -- 11 million people -- have no workplace pension.

Public pensions are good in their design, but governments chose decades ago to keep benefits low.

If ordinary citizens in North America are asked to be responsible for their own pensions regarding retirement why are most politicians voting themselves gold-plated pension plans that are financed by tax payers?

LIFETIME PENSIONS TO LIFETIME WORK

Is it possible to change the traditional late-life model of withdrawal and entitlement into a new paradigm?

POST-RETIREMENT CAREERS

Many individuals either want to or will need to work after retirement. According to an AARP survey, 80 per cent of the baby boom generation intends to continue working after retirement.

What jobs will be available?

Do you begin your own small business as a senior entrepreneur?

Do you give back through community service and participating in an encore non-profit career?

In his book, Colonel Sanders said, "I like to talk to older folks, too. I guess I can speak with authority to them, because I'm older than most of them. Recently I was asked to testify before a House of Representatives special subcommittee that was studying the problems of aging citizens. I told them that in the Garden of Eden God didn't tell Adam that he should work just to retirement age. He said in Genesis 3:19 a man should work 'till thou return unto the ground'- that is, until he died."

And Sanders went on to say something about corporations, "I don't believe that if we can afford it we should rely on loafin'. Life don't have to be easy to be wonderful. Of course, the way large corporations work today, many folks are forced to stop workin' when they reach a certain age. I don't think that's good, but that's the way it is."

The thoughts of an active and productive retirement life were also expressed by authors David Bogan and Keith Davies in the book "Avoid Retirement and Stay Alive" when they said, "Instead of retiring we should keep on living."

They equate retirement with vegetating and waiting for death. The authors also remind us that in earlier days people worked till they died -- that is the pattern that they would like to see replicated today.

One must consider the implications of physical ill health and mental deterioration affecting a significant number of older people -- especially past the age of 80.

The definition of success is changing for baby boomers according to an article in "Money" magazine based on the results of a recent nationwide American survey.

"Boomers are starting to form a **new agenda**, a reinvention of the American dream that emphasizes friends and family over making money, having fun over working hard and making a difference in the community and the world, " said Marlys Harris in her article on the survey.

Nearly 3,000 boomers participated in the survey. The full story appears in the October 2009 issue of the magazine found online at www.cnnmoney.com.

Seniors before retirement concentrate on accomplishments and they work hard in order to achieve goals.

However, when these goals are realized, they don't seem so important anymore.

Pursuing self-actualization means that what you are doing has a purpose at a level that goes far beyond just you or your company. Enlightened and empowered seniorpreneurs expand his or her capacity to create the life they want that benefits themselves and the people they care about – as well as society in general.

Working joyfully in tandem with your true desires and talents you will find yourself thinking:

Is it really this easy?

"I can have fun, make money, and make a difference too!"

CREATIVE RETIREMENT

The desired goal for seniors that want to be successful entrepreneurs should be Maslow's self-actualization level -- fulfilling your highest potential to do good for themselves and society. Seniorpreneurs need to be at these higher levels to achieve creative retirement.

Most seniors are stuck at the lower levels. On fixed incomes these lower level seniors can only hope for basic shelter and basic subsistence.

SELF-ACTUALIZATION

Maslow believed that man has a natural drive to healthiness -- self-actualization. Maslow says there are two processes necessary for this to happen: self-exploration and action. The deeper the self-exploration, the closer one comes to self-actualization.

EIGHT WAYS TO ACTUALIZE

1. Experience things fully, vividly, and selflessly.

   Throw yourself into the experiencing of something: concentrate on it fully – let it totally absorb you.

2. Life is an ongoing choice between safety (out of fear) and risk (for personal growth). **Make the growth choice a dozen times a day.**
3. Let the self emerge. Try to shut out the external clues as to what you should think, feel, say, and so on, and **let your experience enable you to say what you truly feel.**
4. **When in doubt, be honest.** If you look into yourself and are honest, you will also take responsibility. Taking responsibility is self-actualizing.
5. Listen to your own tastes. **Be prepared to be unpopular.**
6. Use your intelligence, **work to do well the things you want to do**, no matter how insignificant they seem to be.
7. Make peak experiencing more likely -- **get rid of illusions and false notions.** Learn what you are good at and what areas need improvement.
8. Find out who YOU are, what you do and don't like, where you are going, and your personal mission. Opening your self up to yourself in this way means identifying

defenses – and then **finding the courage to give them up.**

RETIREMENT ACTIVITIES

Income is obviously one of the major limiting factors with regard to the retirement lifestyle. For instance, studies have shown that when pre-retirees are asked what they would most like to do in retirement, they say travel.

On this same question I personally took a very small poll and found out that travel came out at the top.

When retirees are asked what they are doing, the most common activity is watching television. Here, my small poll indicated that volunteering was the top choice for what they are doing.

"My wife quilts and each year she donates them to the University Hospital who give them to people undergoing treatment for depression. Apparently these people find solace and comfort in a quilt.

I like to mess about in my little workshop making wooden toys for both inner city kids and for an agency that works with slow learner children and their parents.

The latter runs a fundraising event each October and my toy donations are raffled off. Last year (2008) my raffled toys generated better than $1,000 in badly needed funds for them."

FINANCIAL PLANNERS

Financial planners have a big influence on how retirees decide to live.

Most financial planners think that seniors can only get external gratification by becoming involved in activities such as a part-time job or volunteer or community work where there's the possibility of some reward.

Also, financial planners feel that when trying new lifestyles, it is extremely important that you do not rush into radical moves -- such as changing your housing, moving into a new community, or even opening a small business.

FINANCIAL SECURITY

Retirement dreams should not be based on personal financial vehicles such as RRSP's because the government isn't responsible for your total financial security.

Seniors must balance income needs -- instead of demanding more entitlements, they could look at opening up a small business. Seniors will want to create something that fits into his or her lifestyle and circumstances.

The goal does not have to be creating huge sums of wealth for themselves and family members.

RETIREES FORCED BACK TO WORK

Faced with mounting bills and debt, retirees are returning to work to make ends meet.

Only about 55% of full-time retirees can afford to pay basic expenses and have little left over for extras according to a survey by Desjardins Financial Security conducted in December 2009.

Among those surveyed, only 27% can cover basic expenses. Close to two-thirds of them earn less than $20,000 a year. More than two in five of them were forced to plunge deeper in debt in the last year. Close to 16% of retirees continue to work.

Detailed analysis conducted by Kean, Van Zandt, and Maupin (1993) suggested that successful business owners share a number of characteristics -- high levels of autonomy, independence, self-reliance, and personal effectiveness.

These traits are common to entrepreneurs of <u>all</u> ages.

FINANCIAL ADVISOR POINT OF VIEW

Sherry Cooper, chief economist at BMO Nesbitt Burns, formulates that in Canada if you retire at age 65 and have no private pension you will need savings of $700,000 to live comfortably until the age of 90.

This is a great financial position for seniors to achieve based on the assumption that those savings by seniors are handled prudently.

However, there is the story of Ian Thiermann and his wife living in San Jose, California.

Like thousands of retirees, charities, and unsuspecting investors, they invested nearly everything in funds connected to Bernie Madoff Securities -- just before the Wall Street financier was busted for running a $50 billion Ponzi scheme.

In a flash the couple's life savings of $738,000 had vaporized.

Ian had to start over at 90 years old taking a $10.00-an-hour job as a supermarket greeter and was forced to survive on government pension cheques and any small savings.

What motivates a 90-year-old senior to gamble all of his life savings in an extremely high-risk investment? Most seniors are not greedy but simply lack financial literacy education.

SOCIAL SECURITY SURVIVAL

Could you survive on social security?

Today one out of five retirees have nothing but government pension.

The following is an article published on "MSN Money". A true story of a gentleman named Karen Raymond.

He receives $955 a month. That cheque is an improvement from last year, when his entitlement was being garnished for an old child support obligation and he was getting just $529 a month.

Maybe being a guy named "Karen" toughened him up.

All he'll say about his unusual name is, "My mother refused to give up her dreams."

He agreed to share with MSN Money readers what living on Social Security has been like for him.

It will give you some idea of the challenges.

Raymond was never a high earner. For a while, he and his late wife managed a 260-unit welfare hotel in downtown Detroit.

A particularly harrowing episode with some crack addicts persuaded them to move to rural northern Michigan, where they ran a housekeeping and lawn-mowing service.

Poor health -- severe emphysema for him and diabetes, cancer, and a heart condition for his wife -- forced them to shutter the business when he was 60.

They worked as cashiers and received disability payments until they qualified for Social Security at age 62.

His wife died in 2005 of a heart attack -- leaving him alone after 27 years of marriage. Today, he watches every penny.

He knows he spent precisely $959.32 in January, $935.15 in February and $694.80 during the first 17 days of March.

WHERE THE CASH GOES

The biggest chunk of his income -- $278 last month -- goes to heating his small house with propane. The electric bill was $70, while trash pickup was $69. Snowplowing cost $75.

His phone and cell bills run $90, while his food bill for himself and his cat, Squeaks, is under $100 a month. Taxes, car insurance, and various medical supplies like the cane he bought last month, make up the rest. Fortunately, he said, his mortgage has been paid off.

"I don't have house payments. I don't think I would survive if I did."

Raymond's life is pretty simple. Once a month he drives his 1992 Grand Am the 40 minutes or so it takes to get to the Goodwill store. Otherwise, he pretty much stays home.

"I don't watch TV. I don't rent movies. I don't go out to dinner."

His entertainment, until recently, consisted largely of reading two local newspapers -- subscriptions that his sister buys him. He also recently broke down and got a $14 per month internet connection. He finally decided to see for himself what the hoopla was about.

"The first night I was up until 3:30 am... The next night I looked up and the sun was coming up."

The internet has been a good distraction from his financial concerns. He worries that something will happen to his aging car, which he can't afford to replace.

The peeling exterior of his home embarrasses him.

"The house needs painting. It's disgusting. It's lowering my neighbors' property values."

It also bothers him that he owes $40,000 to various local medical providers -- thanks to his wife's illnesses and his own care. He qualified for Medicare last year.

He refuses to file for bankruptcy to wipe out the debt, hoping he'll find some way to pay.

"I might file for bankruptcy if it were corporations... But these are local folks."

If he could pass one bit of advice to younger people, it would be:

"Save. Even if you just start off with a little bit."

Raymond believes people who spend entire working lives getting paid by the hour are often intimidated by the financial world and the advice they hear.

"You have to save six months salary in an emergency fund and it seems like there's no way they can do that. They don't save anything at all."

POOR SENIOR

Raymond does not show any passion to improve his quality of retirement life. As a result, he seems to have no interest in creating profit, or improving his power status, from the present lower level of basic existence.

He is not motivated, not curious, and does not want to take a risk to be more creative and productive. Conquering defeat was not a major consideration.

SENIORS RHYTHM

Seniors want to find a natural retirement life rhythm. Some comments from individual seniors are:

"We have already talked about retirement priorities avoiding naps and going to bed at a regular time, eating properly, etc. However, I am looking forward to spur of the moment plans that are impossible for me now."

"My day always starts the same way. I make coffee, turn the computer on, answer my e-mails and open my own blog. My next activity is whatever project I have set for myself for the day. Today it's house cleaning as I am giving a dinner party Saturday night. I need to pace myself now."

Another retiree needed about ten years or so before he actually retired internally. He was jumping from one major project to another for a long time. Eventually, he found a good rhythm to his day with sailing, computer time, and 'small doses of people'.

These seniors are not willing to extend themselves and find a unique purpose.

Other seniors have developed some bad attitudes after being kind of forced to take part-time jobs after retirement.

"I've been retired over two years and haven't found my rhythm yet. I have taken part-time jobs working at a vitamin store and teach homebound students and have done some traveling.

I also work at the polls during elections. I'm not taking care of my health like I need to and don't get regular exercise and don't eat as well as I should."

This senior has lost control -- frustrated and depressed instead of being full of life working on a life mission.

"I'm still looking for my rhythm. I think I have a half-rhythm. I golf two or three days a week. I find I'm watching my mother and observe how she handles her life.

I'm terrified of the idea of dying, but I did build a website devoted to final resting places."

VULNERABLE SENIORS

Why do so many seniors get swindled?

Natalie L. Denburg and Lyndsay Harshman suggest that vulnerability to scams among some older adults is not part of healthy aging and not a sign of Alzheimer's disease. It is rather a result of abnormalities in specific brain circuits that we rely on for complex decision-making.

A recent theory called the 'Frontal Lobe Hypothesis' by R. West, proposes that some older people have disproportionate age-related changes in frontal lobe structures and the cognitive abilities associated with those structures.

Although decision-making abilities often decline as we get older, Natalie Denburg argues that we should not consider such deficits to be part of normal aging. Denburg suggests that some older adults experience flawed emotional responses that stem from abnormalities that develop in the brains prefrontal cortex.

SENIOR CONSUMERISM

Boomers say their generation has changed the world for the worse when it comes to world peace and poverty. This condition will continue if boomers focus on increased consumerism and entitlements as they enter old age.

We must change this paradigm from wasted consumerism to seniors becoming more productive.

More productivity will lead to more joy and more independence.

It could also create more peace in the world by striking a better balance between the rich and the poor.

HEALTH CARE COVERAGE ISSUE

Whether or not you are sufficiently covered by health care is probably the leading issue of concern when determining to what extent life your later years can be improved.

There are many potential seniorpreneurs who are wasting away at dead-end jobs but cannot break free because of the need for health care.

If you are spending time doing what you don't love, this produces more stress that leads to health problems and a vicious self-defeating cycle.

Basic health coverage is a human right for everyone. It is important that all seniors put more pressure on local and federal governments for more fairness -- especially concerning pre-existing medical conditions.

How are we going to achieve a solution when medical costs today are rising exponentially? We will need to put more emphasis on healthy living and more programs to promote preventive health care.

LOW INCOME HOUSING

Nora retired at the age of 60. Despite losing money in 1999 during a market decline, she was still in decent shape.

"I knew that I had retired a little bit early and that it was probably going to be a tough road at the end, but I thought I was OK."

Recent financial woes have continued to erode her investment savings, and Nora knows she can't continue with bills that add up to approximately $2,000 per month.

When she looked into low-income housing, she found herself stuck between eligibility and livability.

"You can't get by with less money unless you're in low-income housing and you can't get in to low-income housing because you make too much."

Advisors have suggested that seniors cut back on living expenses, consider part-time jobs and utilize financial advisors -- especially when it comes to adjusting future expectations of what your money can do.

SENIORS AND FINANCIAL HARDSHIPS

Does an older population necessarily lead to massive social upheaval and financial hardship?

Many countries are experiencing fiscal crisis, economic stagnation and ugly political battles over entitlements and immigrations.

Greying means paying. More for pensions, more for health care, more for nursing homes for the frail elderly. Yet the benefit systems of most developed countries are already pushing the limits of fiscal and economic affordability. By the 2020s, political warfare over brutal benefit cuts or raising the age for benefit qualification seems unavoidable.

Most of us do not wish upon our children and grandchildren an exorbitant financial burden for elder care in the future. As a result, we desperately need **right now** some more creative, productive solutions. Seniors participating in lifelong learning initiatives and then developing some new ideas for successful business ventures can reduce financial hardships.

This will reduce the demand for benefit entitlements and increase the nest egg income for a lot of the empowered seniors.

RETIREMENT RESCUE PLAN

In America, only 35% of households headed by someone aged 75 or older own any stock at all, compared to 63% of households headed by people between 55 and 64.

It's not surprising that those aged 50 to 70 are the most likely to be hastily rewriting their retirement plans.

They own more equities and may also have been counting on shrinking home equity as a backstop in retirement.

"The recently retired are the most nervous group, but the pre-retirees are beginning to realize that in many cases retirement plans need to change," says Timothy Wyman, a partner with the Center for Financial Planning in Southfield, Michigan.

Financial Planners generally advise retirees to work longer due to investments in a current meltdown.

The other advised strategy is to conserve your cash -- particularly if you are fully or partly retired and can't ramp up earnings.

Unfortunately, financial planners rarely advise that a retiree could also become an entrepreneur and work on something exciting that can be drawn from your own circumstances.

Besides having the chance to write off business expenses by setting up a small business, there is also the possibility of producing a **significant profit margin** based on your own efforts.

Chapter 3
Dare to Dream

"Man has a natural drive to healthiness, of self-actualization. There are two processes for self-actualization: self-exploration and action. The deeper the self-exploration, the closer one comes to self-actualization."

- Maslow (1954)

ENTREPRENEURIAL PREPARATION

In preparation for becoming a senior entrepreneur and for successful aging it is very important to consider and study active brain activities. Richard Restak, a neurologist, said that, "Aging can be thought of as the result throughout the body of a general wear-and-tear process.

In all body organs except the brain, increased activity leads to more wear and tear and accelerated degeneration. In the brain the principle of operation is unique.

Activation of nerve cells doesn't lead to a general degeneration of function but, instead, to the maintenance of neurons during normal aging.

This is really quite an extraordinary situation if you think about it: the brain in contrast to every other organ in the body, has the potential to **improve with use and to keep that edge into the ninth decade and beyond.**

During his research for the book "Older and Wiser", Dr. Restack interviewed many people who are aging successfully and asked them what advice they would give to others. The interviewees were all 70 years of age or older and still productive. From these interviews Dr. Restak extracted ten factors mentioned most often by his subjects as keys to successful aging.

Dr. Restack discovered that the factors mentioned by his subjects as promoting good mental and emotional health match up with factors known to be important in the preservation of peak brain functioning.

1. **Education**

There is an educational opportunity out there – a chance to deepen and learn. It's so sad to see older people retiring to a life of golf, mindless travel, or incessant 'busyness'.

2. **Curiosity**

This is an integrative and complex function related to motivation, arousal, attention, and preference for novelty.

All of these depend upon the operation of the brain at its highest levels of performance.

3. Energy

The challenge in the later years is to generate the same amount of energy you did when you were younger. Sometimes, the best approach to replenishing one's energy reserves is a nap or quiet rest.

4. Keeping Busy

The more things I do that I enjoy doing, the better I feel. As an added bonus you don't have time to brood about the past or get depressed.

5. Regular Exercise

By our 80s most of us have to make some concessions to the state of our physical health. Increased physical activity increases the blood and oxygen supply to the brain by maintaining the health of the blood vessels in the path from heart to the brain.

6. Acceptance

Health in the higher age group isn't perfect. Whatever medical conditions you have to accept them with reasonable normality and continue your life. Acceptance demands a balanced approach to life that not every older person achieves. Ideally these undesired changes could be accepted and incorporated into new behavioral patterns.

7. Diversity and Novelty

To remain mentally sharp, you must develop real interests, not just hobbies. The scale of the activity doesn't matter.

What's important is that the interests involve stimulation -- things to do and achieve as well as a new focus of interest.

8. Linkage and Continuity

By retaining links with the past, we live again through the exercise of our imagination. Revisit many of the places from your childhood and give yourself an opportunity to relive the past.

9. Friends and Social Networks

Your life consists of more than yourself and your immediate surroundings. You have been enriched by your connections with lives other than your own and places different from your present location.

10. Maintaining Links with the Young

We gain by remaining in contact with the thoughts of younger people.

Furthermore, Dr. Restak gives us a take-home message when it comes to the brain -- **your brain: use it or lose it**. After Dr. Restak's research and interviews he became convinced that providing our brain with challenges and stimulation such as entrepreneurial activities is not only desirable but also mandatory if we wish to enjoy a long and healthy life.

SENIORS MINDSET
SENIORS BUSINESS ACTIVITY

A new Ipsos Reid study of Canadian boomers who have retired early to start businesses or intend to do so finds that some 15% of boomer entrepreneurs intend to operate his or her business until they die.

It also appears that boomers want to stay active in the retirement years, with four in ten indicating that they need to keep busy as the reason why they intended to or have started a business.

Other reasons include fulfilling a life-long dream (29 per cent), needing the money (26 per cent), or just a general inclination between themselves and partners to start a business.

Three in ten indicate that they will become or are currently involved in consulting, while retail (13 per cent), entertainment (4 per cent) and hospitality (4 per cent) are other sectors in which boomers are starting businesses.

The new paradigm of increasing entrepreneurial activity with a focus on business training for seniors through lifelong learning programs will raise this group to the next level of self-actualization. The real objective is to utilize vast experience, education, and wisdom to invent more useful products or services for the benefit of themselves and the rest of society.

Boomers are staying with traditional businesses such as consulting, retail, entertainment, and hospitality. However, we really need to get senior entrepreneurs to move to the next higher level and be involved with more prosperous businesses with the potential to hire workers and be able to contribute more to the local economy and society.

COGNITIVE SKILLS

Thomas N. Deuning (2010) focused on the cognitive skills that successful entrepreneurs possess:

1. The opportunity-recognizing mind.
2. The designing mind.
3. The risk-taking mind.
4. The resilient mind.
5. The effectuating mind.

These five minds provide an intellectual foundation for entrepreneurship, education, and curriculum development.

Seniors are being wrongly stereotyped as grouchy, inflexible, and unhappy people living in nursing homes.

This is incorrect according to Canadian researchers.

"It's important to base our interactions upon the person in front of us and specific abilities as opposed to relying on stereotypes and possibly incorrect knowledge," says Tiana Rust, the lead author of a study from the University of Alberta.

About 60 per cent of the people questioned said adaptability was rare or present in about half of older people, but studies have shown most seniors have a willingness to change.

41 percent of caregivers and 19 percent of

students thought joy was less common in the elderly than younger people.

Research has shown that happiness is just as common in the elderly.

Almost 40 percent of those questioned thought 25 per cent of people over 65 lived in institutions but the actual number is about five per cent.

When it came to questions about aging in general, the two groups had nearly equal scores.

The students got 39 percent right, while caregivers fared little better at 40 percent.

The low numbers indicate that there is definitely room to move upward in terms of levels of knowledge.

As our population is aging it is going to become more and more important to correctly assess this situation.

SENIORS CURIOSITY

A sense of curiosity is required for seniors when learning or thinking about the future.

Bern, a 95-year-old senior says, "People my age, most of them don't have any curiosity. They either know it all or they don't want to know it all."

Furthermore, Bern doesn't see an old man when he looks in the mirror. He feels 75 and is determined to live that way.

"What is old? It's a state of mind," Bern says.

Denis Rhyme and his wife have been retired more than twelve years now and neither of them have time to be bored.

Denis says that "I am less than a year from the big 80. My hobbies are computers, writing poetry and essays, and running a small forum for like-minded individuals.

I also stay on top of a two-acre garden with more than 50 flower beds, a large fish pond full of goldfish, and three reflecting ponds.

We also have two small dogs that we walk three times daily for a couple of kilometers. This keeps us both busy from the time we rise at 6:00 am -- long time habits are hard to break -- until we retire at 10:30 pm."

Sharon, a 65 year old, says that she would ideally like to work four days a week. On her day off Sharon runs around like a lunatic doing chores and such and she's contemplating activities such as volunteering but hasn't committed herself to a project yet.

The traits common here are procrastination and no serious goals for a productive retirement life.

COMMUNITY SERVICE ACTIVITIES

Will Baby Boomers actually work in retirement to serve the community and those in need?

Princeton Survey Research Associates International in 2005 found the following:

1. 78% are interested in working to help the poor, the elderly, and other people in need.
2. 56% are interested in dealing with health issues -- working in a hospital or with an organization fighting a particular disease.
3. 55% are interested in a teaching or other educational position.

4. 45% say they are interested in working in a youth program.

And more boomer women than men (50% to 28%) say the opportunity to help people in need is a very important characteristic attracting them to a job in retirement.

Is everybody going to aspire to becoming a community organizer like Barrack Obama did prior to his election to office?

North Americans aged 50 to 70 are ready now to pitch in and help with challenges facing their communities in the areas of education, health care, or caring for those in need.

LIFELONG LEARNING OPPORTUNITIES

Should the traditional senior centres or any future boomer centres need to change by updating the functions and activities offered?

A recent Associated Press story put it in black and white: "Susan Lather envisions a day when patinas and mocha cocktails will take their place next to fruit cups and club sandwiches on the lunch menu at the Enfield Senior Centre. Changing food preferences are among many adjustments that Senior Centre directors nationwide, including Lather, expect to make in the next decade as they balance the wishes of their elderly stalwarts with those of baby boomer newcomers."

Future boomer centres should focus more on entrepreneurial business and encore non-profit subjects that are organized around the mission of lifelong learning. Presently, courses taken such as 'History of Ancient Rome' or watercolor classes could be complemented with job search, business incubators, and skills workshops.

There will always be a practical use for senior centres because a lot of people including boomers will not want to pursue either encore non-profit careers or entrepreneurial projects. Lifelong learning centres can he created exist along side the traditional senior centres. However, current senior centres will just serve the lowest common denominator -- providing lower energy kind of activities and functions. For more enhanced social engagement we will need new locations offering more creative solutions.

There was an interesting comment by John Keyon on the Internet regarding the topic of lifelong learning centres when he said, "I agree Joe.

Interesting that you mention the need for new locations.

Whenever I travel to other cities' civic centers, 1 usually see a senior centre sign with an arrow pointing away from City Hall -- usually to a remote location.

I think that's indicative of current society's view of senior involvement.

The preference is to recognize that seniors exist, but let's keep them from civic engagement.

It reminded me of what we do with locating prisons away from population centers, and may send a subtle message that seniors are social outcasts.

At least that's one interpretation of why they are often remotely located."

GENERATIONS ONLINE – SENIORS AND THE INTERNET

"Wired seniors -- internet users aged 65 or older -- are often cited as the fastest-growing demographic group online, but that description can be misleading.

Most of the growth in this group over the last few years has come from long-time internet users in their early sixties aging into senior status. There is little evidence that many non-users in their seventies and eighties are suddenly getting the internet bug."

- Pew Internet & American Life, "Are Wired Seniors Sitting Ducks?", April 2006

Generations Online -- the non-profit program for internet literacy and access for the elderly, estimates some 21 million people over 65 do not and will not ever use the internet -- unless we intervene.

Only 34% of the 34.5 million Americans over the age of 65 use the internet.

Only 28% of Americans age 70 and older go online -- compared to 73% of all Americans online.

A possible suggestion here is to provide more suitable computer and internet courses as part of a lifelong learning opportunity strategy. For example, seniors could learn to be more computer literate to enable participation in online discussion forums.

In order to encourage more entrepreneurial activities by seniors, we will need more business-oriented courses to be included as a lifelong learning opportunity strategy.

Wayne Harrigan said, "In southeastern New Brunswick we have a new program starting called the Tantramar Seniors College. It's non-profit and will involve retirees teaching other retirees.

A similar program has been running in Prince Edward Island for a few years, and it is doing very well. Courses here will run three terms in a year -- winter, spring and fall.

One membership fee of $100.00 will allow students to take as many courses as they would like -- including Intro to Computers, Memoir Writing, Digital Photography, Vegetarian cooking, Music Appreciation, Bridge for Beginners, Watercolor, Creative Writing, French Conversation, Quilting, Beginner Ukulele, Curling, and Reupholstering. "

Also, in my hometown of Edmonton we have Minerva Senior Studies Institute. The mission of Minerva is to provide learning opportunities for adults fifty and over by developing, sponsoring, promoting, offering, and participating in educational activities designed to enhance seniors intellectual pursuits.

Minerva Senior Studies undertakes to:

- Promote lifelong learning.
- Extend educational access to seniors.

- Deliver a sound senior-friendly volunteer program.
- Be innovative and responsive in program planning and evaluation.
- Be fiscally responsible.
- Share expertise and demonstrate leadership in educational initiatives.

For more info on courses check out the website www.minerva.macewan.ca.

SENIORS TRAINING PROGRAMS

There is the possibility that some problems do exist regarding setting up training programs for seniors. Studies at Monash University in Australia found that 80% of Australians leave the workforce by the age of 65 and only 5% of Australians are still working at the age of 70.

Older workers are facing barriers to participation in skills development training programs, including employer attitudes, a lack of information about training options being provided to them, work and family commitments, financial difficulties, and sometimes their own doubts about their ability to succeed.

DO COMPUTERS INTIMIDATE SENIORS?

According to Neilson, those ages 65 and over still only make up less than 10 percent of active internet users.

In a five year period, the number of active internet seniors has increased from 11.3 million users in 2004 to 17.5 million in 2009. This shows that there is a significant increase in the number of seniors using computers.

Are seniors maximizing their opportunities or do they just perform basic operations and minimal computer research?

Seniors do not seem to be intimidated by computers. Still, we need to find out why at a seniors website, such as seniorsdaily.net, there only 5 – 10 active forum members out of 800 active members.

Seniors seem to be afraid to express their own opinions.

According to Nielsen, seniors are spending more time on the internet – an average of about 52 hours a month in 2004 compared to 58 hours in 2009.

What are they doing on the web?

Seniors are mostly e-mailing, paying bills, checking weather, planning trips, or learning about health, politics, or business.

These types of usage are personal ones. As a result, one possible solution to helping seniors become more computer literate is to provide lifelong learning computer courses.

This would enable seniors to become more active, productive, and creative in retirement life.

Seniors could also have the opportunity to do some creative writing and with the invention of the iPad and Kindle, a new future could be opened up to seniors.

SENIOR SUPPORT NETWORK

The concept of a support network for seniors who are beginning to start second-life activities will be very important for the baby boomer generation.

This network hopefully will be available on the Internet to support collaboration, creativity, and innovation.

Also, all seniors need to increase their computer and financial literacy to get the most benefit in their retirement life.

Furthermore, I know that there are many boomers (people born between 1946 and 1964) and zoomers (boomers and non-boomers with a zip -- people aged 40 - 80) that would be interested in taking some challenging business and leadership programs.

This takes into consideration the goal of contributing more to society through life-long learning, as compared to the need to make a pile of easy money from very risky investments.

Because of the increasing number of boomers reaching retirement age, there are a significant number of people desiring to be more creative and productive. If some business support groups were created for seniors they could provide a visible network of like-minded individuals to discuss their mutual problems and successes.

This could bring to the table some new ideas to inspire seniors to become more active and productive in society.

We know that there are seniors out there that want to pursue their own secret talent just like Colonel Sanders did.

Even Obama is calling boomers to action as he said, "Seniors getting ready to retire is a crucial source of new ideas that could benefit millions of Americans if they're given the chance to grow."

He endorsed social entrepreneurship as a significant public policy by calling for a Social Investment Fund Network to invest in ideas that work; leveraging private sector dollars to encourage innovation; and expanding successful programs to scale.

Just as small business administration provides support for small companies, a new Social Entrepreneur Agency would muster federal support for small non-profits.

He also added that federal support could be available for seniors that decide to set up small businesses. This would encourage entrepreneurial activities among seniors.

The same case can be made for giving seniors life-long learning opportunities to become successful entrepreneurs, which would help seniors to become financially independent.

SENIORS INVESTING KNOWLEDGE

Boomers do not appear to be particularly

experienced with investing, as roughly two-thirds consider themselves to be beginners. Additionally, fewer than 20 per cent consider themselves to be very knowledgeable when it comes to investing for retirement.

Because of many strange marketing practices, financial advisors are in some cases making more money than the common investor.

In general, financial advisors tend to market retirement planning through a soft-sell approach they call lifestyle planning, heavy on suggestions that you should travel to an exotic country or take some tennis lessons.

This focus is on being a consumer rather than choosing to live a creative, productive retirement life with activities such as writing books, inventing new products and services, or painting a prize-winning work of art.

Abstract painter Carmen Herrera of New York City -- after six decades of very private painting -- sold her first piece five years ago at the age of 89.

Now, at a ceremony in her honor in her loft apartment, she basked in the realization that her career had finally taken off.

As cameras flashed, she accepted **an art foundation lifetime achievement** award. Since the first sale in 2004, collectors have avidly pursued Herrera, and her radiantly aesthetic paintings now sell for $30,000 US.

Canadian Business Magazine in the December 7, 2009 issue had an article by Joe Castaldo titled "Are you getting too old to invest on your own?"

Some economists have concluded that financial decision-making skills begin to decline in middle age at 53 years old.

As a result, the authors suggest a government licensing system be instituted to ensure older adults have a base level of financial understanding before they are permitted to invest.

I agree there is a need for government or private corporation sponsorship to create and develop financial education that is targeted and useful for seniors.

However, financial advisors and companies must also take some responsibility for selling debatable products such as sub-prime mortgages and the chaos triggered around the world when clients could no longer make payments.

When financial advisors state that "nobody

forced anybody to do anything" or "investors need to be more attentive", the whole story is not being told.

Overzealous sales representatives and product hype that is sometimes less than truthful sold sub-prime mortgages and high-interest home equity loans.

Chapter 4
Do I Need a Business Plan?

"What happens if you try to build a house on a weak foundation? The house eventually cracks or caves in. Before you build a big house you must build a solid foundation. The business equivalent to building a solid foundation is called 'creating a system'. A business system is a repeatable process that produces a profit."

- T. Harv Eker, Speedwealth, 2001

peakpotentials.com

This is the **first step in attracting investors.** Every startup business needs a solid business plan and expert advice to create it.

Entrepreneurship can be one of the most rewarding experiences of your life. It can also be filled with challenges.

You first need to evaluate yourself to see if you have the necessary attitudes, abilities, and experiences to succeed in running your own small business.

While there are many personal attributes that make up a successful entrepreneur, there are three areas in which they all seem to shine:

1. They know just who they are as well as personal strengths and weaknesses
2. They make creative thinking part of their daily habits
3. They set goals and follow them. They have a **vision of where they are going** and have **developed the <u>plans</u>** they need to make goals a reality.

TAKING INVENTORY

All entrepreneurs are optimistic. The successful ones are realistic. Being an independent business person places great demands on you. You are the business – the originator, its motivating force, and energy.

A lot of people start a business without ever completing an honest, thorough personal inventory. They make the mistake of narrowing choices too quickly and start the first business that comes to mind.

Without honest self-appraisal, personal success in business can be difficult.

Defining what you are selling is based on your understanding of the business. A lot of small businesses fail to properly define exactly what business they are doing and consequently find it very difficult to tell people what it is they are selling.

It sounds very simple, but it is often difficult to pin down unless you take a good look at all the aspects of the business you are pursing. Knowing exactly what product or service you are selling is very important. Being able to define your product or service in a few words is never easy. For example, Colonel Sanders' product is the eleven herbs and spices secret recipe for fried chicken.

FIVE STEPS

1. **Assessment:** Generate or develop your ideas, evaluate the business potential, and find out if running a business is for you.

2. **Business Plan:** an essential tool to plan, finance, and market your business

3. **Starting Up:** Choosing a name, hiring an accountant and a lawyer, and legal obligations

4. **Financing:** Find financing for your business as well as links to additional funding
5. **First-year:** Managing day to day operations and planning your company's growth

"The fundamentals do not spring forth, self-evident and active, from the brow of every former grocery clerk, soda jerk, military man, or specialist in one of the hundreds of other callings who join the ranks of McDonald's operators.

Quite the contrary; the basics have to be stressed over and over. The operators need the stress on fundamentals as much as the managers and crews."

- Ray Kroc, Founder of McDonalds, *Grinding It Out – The Making of McDonalds*

WRITING YOUR BUSINESS PLAN

Now that you have completed your business planning, the next step is assembling all the information you have gathered.

It will now take all the information you have developed to create your business plan.

THE ONE PERSON BUSINESS

If you are going to be the sole owner and worker in the business, it is important that you describe your company as being related to your own experience and abilities – clearly identifying that the strength of the company is in what you bring to it.

Show how your past experience, abilities, and skills fit in with your business plans. Often when the company is a sole proprietor, you can weave your own expertise into the company description.

This is acceptable because the company is really you and relies on your strengths. If there is more than one player in the business, determine the strengths each will bring to the company.

BUSINESS PLAN PREPARATION

Many business owners are often too close to their own businesses and prepare a business plan that is too subjective and leaves out important financial considerations.

Because every successful startup business needs a solid business plan, it is advisable to hire a professional business planner.

Coaching and mentoring services will be required to produce the first business plan and provide everyday guidance in managing the plan.

Mentors can also suggest ways that this plan could be made more effective in meeting the seniorpreneur goals and objectives for a successful business.

If financial investors were required anytime during the life of the startup business, a coach or mentor would be there to advise how much money is required to finance any stage of this business and to ensure that the business will have full growth opportunities for the future.

As an entrepreneur, there will be no one telling you what to do or how to do it. So it will be important to work with other people who can help you get your business started.

They may be partners, accountants, mentors, lawyers, coaches or others.

Within your overall business plan there will be an operations plan, marketing plan and a financial plan.

Sometimes to simplify things it is useful to include an action planner and an overall schedule for the start up of your business.

I attended an action-planning workshop at the Microbusiness Training Centre. They provide guidance in the areas of inspiration, planning, coaching, and mentoring for entrepreneurs. More info can be found at: www.microbusiness.ca.

The action planner schedule should outline the timing and relationship of the major events that are necessary to get your business going.

The schedule is a planning aid and shows deadlines. It is also an effective sales tool for raising money from potential investors.

A well-prepared and realistic schedule shows preparation for growth in a way that accounts for obstacles and lessens risks.

Your schedule must outline the timing of activities such as product development, market planning, sales programs, and operations.

There needs to be enough detail to show how much time will be required to accomplish each major goal.

Dates of deadlines and milestones necessary for your business success should include some of the following:

- Incorporation
- Ordering of sufficient materials for full-time operation
- Tenant improvements or renovations
- Start of operation or opening of store
- Receipt of first customer orders
- First sales and deliveries as it relates to your business credibility and need for capital
- Launch of the marketing plan

Often we tend to underestimate the time it takes to do things, so be realistic about your schedule.

An **action planner worksheet** can be found on www.seniorpreneur.ca.

CREATING A MARKETING PLAN

To stay in business you must be able to reach your customers. To reach your customers, you need an effective marketing plan.

It is vital to your business success that you contact and motivate customers.

However, it costs money to make money, so it is very important that your marketing strategy is carefully and thoughtfully designed.

INTRODUCE YOURSELF AND YOUR COMPANY

Who are you and what do you do?

You have only a few seconds to create your first impression when you meet someone and only a few words to communicate exactly what it is you can offer.

What would you say when someone asks you to describe your business? Before you can properly promote yourself and your business, you **must** have an answer to this question.

You need to understand the importance of creating a first impression that represents what you have to offer. You should be able to sum it up in less than 25 words.

Instead of "I'm an artist" you need to define your art and business:

"I am an artist who specializes in miniature paintings using acrylic on canvas. I sell these paintings through a number of local craft stores."

If you want to include your company name,

add ten words:

"I am the owner of Expressions Gallery. Our company specializes in producing miniature paintings using acrylic on canvas. We sell these paintings through a number of local craft stores."

More marketing strategies will be presented and discussed in **Chapter 6: Caution -- Exhaustion Ahead?**

CREATING A FINANCIAL PLAN

In a majority of cases seniorpreneurs will need some start up capital.

Sources of new business funding include equity financing, debt financing, and venture capital financing.

My business partner and I presented a business plan for our company specializing in the purchase of bakery and restaurant food equipment and supplies.

I had very limited resources and my business partner possessed cash, vehicle, and bakery food equipment assets.

The specific problem was that our bank loan requirements did not provide enough business assets collateral to satisfy the bank.

My business partner had other personal assets such as real estate and some used bakery equipment.

He decided not to commit his personal assets as security for the loan.

FINANCING OPTIONS

- Chartered banks
- Credit Unions
- Third-party investors (angel and venture capital financing)
- Friends, family
- Vendor finance if purchasing an existing business

The following are tips and suggestions offered by Heather McLeod, Account Manager, Business Development Corporation (BDC).

More information can be obtained at www.bdc.ca.

TIPS FOR SELECTING A BANKER

- What experience do they have in your sector?
- What is their loan approval level?
- Can they negotiate rate and terms?
- What is your personal track record or experience with them?

WHAT BANKING SERVICES ARE YOU SHOPPING FOR?

- Operating Loan or Line of Credit
- Term Loans for expansion or renovation
- Loans to Purchase Assets
- Interest-bearing Deposits for Cash
- VISA or MC Merchant Account
- VISA or MC Expense Account
- What is a personal guarantee?

HOW TO MAINTAIN A GOOD BANKING RELATIONSHIP

- don't hide problems

- establish a reputation for integrity
- adhere to bank policy
- provide financial information
- invite your banker 'in' to your business
- schedule regular meetings

WHY LOANS GET TURNED DOWN

- Outside this bank's policy
- Too Risky or Unsound
- Insufficient Collateral
- Poor Business Plan
- Purpose of the loan not clear

WHY LOANS GET APPROVED

- your familiarity with the business
- your ability to pay back debt
- your ability to provide security
- your level of equity
- secondary sources to repay debt

- how much money for how long, for what
- your integrity
- your businesslike approach
- your judgement
- your personal appearance
- your credit rating
- your lead-time (so talk to us early!)

Traditionally, a large volume of angel and venture capital financing is only available for wealthy individuals requiring loans in the range of $1 to 2 million. Often these loans are traded for convertible or common stock shares.

In most cases this financing option is out of reach for most start up senior entrepreneurs.

We have seniors that want to be seniorpreneurs and we will have successful senior entrepreneurs who desire to help those in the startup phase or the growth phase of personal business ventures.

The goal of each community is often to develop the best economic situation possible.

The successful senior entrepreneurs could

act as mentors and coaches. Also, they could provide angel and venture capital financing options for the startup or growth seniorpreneurs.

This strategy would promote and spread a movement of seniors helping seniors.

The business risk could be reduced because in your own community there is the option of getting more face to face networking opportunities.

It's a win-win scenario because the mentor benefits by becoming a social entrepreneur and the seniorpreneur grows with the mentor's entrepreneurial knowledge and some angel financing.

Chapter 5
Dreaming Big, Starting Small

DAVE'S ADVICE TO SENIORS

Dreaming big yet starting small is easier said than done. Dave Thomas, founder of Wendy's, offers the following from his book "Dave's Way":

Don't retire... age is just a number.

I'm really against seniors retiring. We have seniors working in our restaurants. The eighteen to twenty-five year old group is the most rapidly shrinking part of the population. That's the age group from which we used to get all of our staff.

We have people in our restaurants who are eighty years old! They're fantastic. They enjoy it. They know all the customers. People who have always been busy probably need to be busy doing something.

One senior told me a few days ago, "You have to have a reason to put your makeup on in the morning and get out of the house."

Do what you want

When I say don't retire that doesn't mean that seniors shouldn't have jobs. More than anything, it's important that senior citizens be in something they really like to do. Some folks join the Peace Corps. Others do community service. Still others go into business on their own. Stay active, but stay active doing what YOU want to do.

Take a walk on the wild side

Colonel Sanders dressed up like he walked off the set of *Gone With the Wind*. Clara "Where's the Beef?" Peller used to give press conferences, even though she couldn't hear the reporter's questions. Grandma Minnie Sinclair would use five or six testers in the perfume department to blend her own personal fragrance in the Saturday trips to the five-and-dime. All the fun seniors I have ever met were a little eccentric.

People are living longer these days. Plenty of people spend twenty to twenty-five years being a "senior citizen". The way I look at it, why not figure out how to do it right off the bat -- when there are just sixty candles on the cake?

BUSINESS STARTUP

Finding your true passion requires you to look inside yourself using your own intuition and creativity to fulfill your destiny. Be internally directed not externally controlled.

Be your own person.

Why do we go to business seminars or workshops to find our dreams?

Business seminars or workshops are generally structured to provide only a skeleton of basic information.

The purpose is to sell attendees very expensive training courses with no guarantee of success.

Seminar leaders want you to look outside yourself to produce results. This is why you'll find many sets of seminar materials purchased then placed on a shelf to be read later. There was no interest to study the subject that was bought from an overzealous sales presenter.

The seminar attendee is only financing the dream of the seminar presenter.

THREE STEPS TO ACHIEVING GOALS

- Write out your plan and constantly expand it.
- Imagine clearly and vividly your plan realized.
- Constantly affirm your plan's perfect fulfillment

Too often we live our lives selecting what we don't want then complain about how much we spent on something we don't want. Make lists of your heart's desire. Be crystal clear what you want and by what date. It's very important to start immediately. Eliminate procrastination, worry, doubt, fear and the negative use of 'How'. Trust in God or Spirit. If you are still afraid maybe Matthew 7:7 will be able to help you- 'Ask and it shall be given you; seek and ye shall find; knock, and it shall be opened unto you'.

WORKING JOYFULLY

Working hard brings with it all the "must do's" and "to do's" plus all the heaviness that those lists entail. Working joyfully brings ease, fun, inspiration, and a light, powerful sense. When you work joyfully, you are working in tandem with spirit, in tandem with your true desires. When you work hard you are usually pushing against something. For example, Colonel Sanders was working in tandem with his spirit and in tandem with his true desires. He developed his "true talent" -- a secret chicken seasoning recipe.

GET READY.

GET SET.

GO!

I turned 65 years old in 2010 -- an ideal age to play the role of a seniorpreneur. Just as an athlete prepares to run an important marathon, seniors can prepare for an encore career or an entrepreneurial project. As you get ready, get set, and start your personal run, the spectators will be standing up and cheering wildly in appreciation for your extraordinary effort.

You approach the finish line confidently with a feeling that you've accomplished as much self-actualization as is humanly possible.

If you had a chance to select a role model or a mentor to give you some personal advice on how to become a successful entrepreneur whom would you choose? I would select Colonel Sanders to be my own personal inspiration story.

Sanders came from a very large, very poor family. When he was 65, as he sat on his front porch, the mailman came up the steps and handed him an envelope. It was from the U.S. government and contained his first Social Security cheque in the amount of $105.

What did the Colonel think about doing now? How did he choose the right product to produce and distribute to the right markets?

Sanders was experimenting with different herbs and spices for many years in his restaurant career. He came to the point where he knew that he had the right combination.

He didn't want to change the recipe any more as it could become less than the best tasting recipe. The Colonel personally drove his station wagon to meet potential clients.

Then he invited his clients to his home where he offered his specialty -- chicken prepared in a pressure cooker.

Restaurant clients were invited for a sleepover where the customers were treated to a hearty country breakfast in the morning, after which business was conducted on a handshake -- a gentlemen's agreement.

The Colonel's second wife, Claudia, prepared the blended secret seasonings at home and packaged the product in bucket containers. At this stage of the business, the planning was kept simple and personal.

The scale of the business was manageable as a home-based business.

For example, he bought individual seasonings from different suppliers, mixed and blended the recipe in standard buckets, and the finished product was taken physically to the local post office for weighing and shipping to distant customers.

After being successful in the business startup stage, the next level – franchising – requires more planning and the ability to handle setbacks. Face your fears, and rely on faith to get you through it.

FACE YOUR FEARS WITH FAITH

So why is an aging society seen solely in terms of increasing dependency?

Is this because traditionally older people did not guard against being negative and apathetic and often expressed the feeling that "nothing can be done?"

You can face your fear by applying four positive principles:

- Have vision
- Have faith
- Put your faith into action
- Allow your spirit to carry you

A lot of seniors face problems of incredible magnitude -- our personal Goliaths. Some are facing the Goliath of unbelief, and the Goliath of negative thinking.

To overcome your Goliath, you first must have a vision.

Believe you can do the impossible.

To overcome your Goliath, you must have faith in your spirit and in your ability.

You can conquer any mountain.

Faith is nothing without action even if you have all the faith in the world.

Put your faith into action and win the battle.

Allow your spirit to carry you.

Give in and let go.

Sanders said, "If I ever needed help from God I needed it now. While I was tithing (that is, givin' a tenth of my income to God's work) and I suppose you would say being a professional Christian, I still knew I wasn't doing altogether right by God. And of course, my cussin was still a big problem with me."

"Now that I had auctioned off my restaurant in Corbin, the idea of franchising my recipe for Kentucky Fried chicken seemed to be the next thing for me to do. And while I wasn't right with God, I remember prayin' to God Almighty — You've helped me in the past, and I need your help now. I promise you, if this idea of franchising works out because of your blessing, you'll get your share."

I believe that your spirit carries you to the point where you're back on our feet again, and then you're able to reach out to others and carry them when they need a hand. Slowly, but surely, you'll be raised to higher ground.

What is your 'secret' talent?

The choice of your product or service should be part of your own circumstances, and not something being imposed upon you from outside influences.

Colonel Sanders said, "You see, you are not startin' out from nothin', but from the point at which you have assimilated the lessons of a lifetime. Those years are sort of the crown you wear as you begin the next phase of your life… I still don't think I've done anythin' special that nobody else couldn't of done if he'd been in the same circumstances."

EUREKA MOMENT

Get out of the rat race!

My particular eureka moment came on August 31, 1990. It was my last day working for the Alberta Liquor Control Board (ALCB) in the Head Office in St. Albert, Alberta. My role was a contract-purchasing officer. The staff on that day had a goodbye luncheon party for me.

I remember getting a pen gift set, saying my last greetings to fellow staff members and then calling a taxi to go home.

As I was traveling back home I made a promise to myself not to look back in the rear view mirror, and just start a new career as a seniorpreneur.

Because my work background was purchasing management and transportation services and research, it made perfect sense for me to set up a purchasing services consulting company – Cost-Effective Purchasing Services.

At first I tried to do everything myself. This experience showed me that a serious new business was impossible without some team members.

I discussed this opportunity with a life long friend and fellow seniorpreneur Tim Visscher.

We changed the company name, added a logo, printed brochures, company letterhead, applications and price lists, and became Dynamic Purchasing Services Inc.

We incorporated this company on February 4, 1994. The company was a home-based business and operated for almost 4 years.

I had one of my WOW moments during this time. Even though we had difficulty generating profit for any of the four years, the business itself was run as a first class operation.

My business partner was also the financing person and I noticed that I was having a lot more joy than he was having.

I was gaining entrepreneurial experience, while my business partner only noticed the drain on his financial resources. At least I felt that NOW I was really on the road out of the rat race, and it would he very difficult to go back to a corporate life job.

Chapter 6
Caution -- Exhaustion Ahead?

Before I ask any more questions in the following chapters, let's talk about a new paradigm assessment tool for seniors.

A legitimate concern expressed about grey entrepreneurs is that they will exhibit lower productivity and energy levels than younger counterparts.

Poor personal health has been suggested as the most common reason older people choose to retire from working life or decline to seek paid employment.

Declines in productivity are more common over the age of 75. Seniors aged 65 – 75 tend to be much more capable of starting a business.

Greater experience and knowledge can balance out these concerns.

Business Development Model For Seniors
Take a personal inventory of self.

Where are you now?

Colonel Sanders took stock of his life at 65 years old and said, "It somehow seemed to me that the recipe I had developed for my Kentucky Fried Chicken (KFC) might be something I could work with…"

Set a goal.

Where do you want to be in the future?

Sanders said, "Now that I had auctioned off my restaurant in Corbin, the idea of franchising my recipe for Kentucky Fried Chicken seemed to be the next thing for me to do."

Identify your skills, passions and interests.

Sanders said, "You are not starting out from nothing but from the point at which you have assimilated the lessons of a lifetime.

Those years are sort of the Crown you wear as you begin the next phase of your life."

Sixth-grade dropout, farmhand, army mule-tender, locomotive fireman, railroad section hand, aspiring lawyer, insurance salesman, ferryboat entrepreneur, chamber of commerce secretary, tire salesman, amateur obstetrician, political candidate, gas station operator, motel operator, and restaurant owner built his Crown of Life.

At the age of 65, a new Interstate highway snatched the traffic away from his corner, and Sanders was left with nothing but a social security cheque and a secret recipe for fried chicken.

That's all he needed!

Clearly identify your dream and use your passions, interests, and resources.

Find a way to make your dreams a reality. How do you get from where you are now to where you want to be?

Develop a marketing plan to take your business to the next level.

Sanders said, "When you are in the restaurant business you're always lookin' out for some kind of specialty dish that you can offer which will prove an attraction to your customers, and yet is something your competitor doesn't have."

Pete Harman of Salt Lake City, Utah was

KFC's first franchisee. He had a large sign on the front window of the restaurant: "Kentucky Fried Chicken -- Something New, Something Different." Pete was so enthusiastic about the chicken he had a commercial running every hour on the local radio station. He also talked about it at the National Restaurant Association conventions. The first freestanding building to sell Kentucky Fried Chicken was put up in Jacksonville, Florida by Wally Desser. It was a model for everything that has been done since.

Don't procrastinate.
Set a deadline for making your dream a reality.

Make wise choices to help you
reach your goal by the deadline.

BAD HABITS

1. Stop working or stop working on a business.
2. Travel for leisure. For example, golfing or tanning on a beach.
3. Live only on social security and some small pension.

4. Attend only passive senior centres.
5. Sitting on a rocking chair watching TV and listening to the radio.
6. Babysitting grand kids full-time.
7. Playing bingo, casino, or horse races.
8. Gathering at shopping mall food courts with the same friends.

GOOD HABITS

1. Start-up a new business or continue previous business.
2. Travel for business purposes.
3. Live on pensions plus business income, cash flow, and royalties.
4. Attend active lifelong learning centres.
5. Meet with clients or prospect for new clients.
6. Visit grand kids at distant places.
7. Play financial education games.
8. Gather at conventions to network and promote business.

Develop a solid foundation to move ahead and think about

different charities and church organizations you will support with your surplus funds.

Sanders said, "Yes I was tryin' to do right by my fellow men. Like I said before, just about all my life I gave my tithe to the church. I was a good Rotarian and a good citizen and all that. But to me, money isn't everything. I was more interested in doing good and helping people."

In 1964, Sanders sold out to a group of investors for $2 million. Besides the $2 million, he received a lifetime salary of $40,000. This was raised to $75,000 to promote the business.

He held on to his Canadian rights in the company and established a foundation in Canada turning over his profits to charities, hospitals, the Boy Scouts, and the Salvation Army. He also adopted 78 foreign orphans. Today, the Colonel Harland Sanders Charitable Organization Inc. still exists in Canada.

CASH IN ON YOUR CREATIVITY

Older entrepreneurs are not calling it quits and heading off for a quiet retirement. As baby boomers grow older, and as people need to work longer in order to continue supplementing their income, we will see an ever-increasing trend of seniorpreneurs starting up new businesses.

Traditionally, government policy has been focused on younger entrepreneurs (18-34). Assuming the boomers take advantage of lifelong learning opportunities, future government policy will need to focus more on seniors and senior entrepreneurs.

The present social networking sites such as Facebook or Twitter serve younger entrepreneurs very well.

On the other hand, many boomer sites like Facebook are not a suitable fit for them.

I now have a Facebook account. However, I was basically against it since I didn't think the site had any business value. I was wrong.

It is possible to focus on developing your own business but you must be aware that there are some people that misuse this website by sending you spam instead of trying to develop a personal relationship.

Also, I use four different social networking sites that are geared more to the seniors demographic – seniorsdaily.net, zoomers.ca, encore.org, and zentrepreneurs.com.

My own website is www.seniorpreneur.ca.

Each of these sites will need strong leadership to empower seniors just to participate actively on a daily basis.

CREATING A MARKETING PLAN

To stay in business you must be able to reach your customers. To reach your customers, you need an effective marketing plan. It is vital to your business that you contact and motivate customers. However, it costs money to make money, so it is very important that your marketing strategy is carefully and thoughtfully designed.

THE FOUR P's OF MARKETING

1. **Product:** the tangible aspects of the product or service itself.
2. **Price:** the cost advantage to the customer or buyer
3. **Place:** access to the product – such as high traffic areas, impulse buys, retail displays, convenient home delivery, or 24 hour on-call.
4. **Promotion:** the amount and nature of the marketing activities associated with a particular product or service.

YOUR COMPANY'S MESSAGE

Every business sends a message in its marketing. The message is a statement of your competitive edge. It emphasizes a quality the company values that sets you apart from the competition. For example, "At Ford, quality is job one." Sometimes, the message describes a market niche. As an example: "Specialists in Estate Planning". Sometimes it is directed at the consumer's self-image: "You deserve a break today." These are often called "positioning statements".

See if you can come with a few that reflect your commitment to your customer. Try to come up with just a few words that "say it all."

HOW SMART MARKETERS WIN BATTLES

1. Research your marketplace.
2. Write a competitive advantage and benefits list.
3. Select the marketing weapons best suited for your attack.
4. Create your marketing plan and focus on the goals and create calendar

5. Make arrangements with fusion marketing.
6. Launch your attack by firing the weapons
7. Maintain the attack, hang in there, win with confidence, plant the seeds
8. Measure your attack and fire your best weapons
9. Improve your attack in all areas, invest less and get more, continuously improve customer satisfaction, manage your moments of truth.

These marketing weapons should all be considered for promoting your product, service or website. Notice how more than **half** of them are *free*.

A list of marketing weapons can be found on www.seniorpreneur.ca.

Chapter 7
PUBLIC POLICY AND AGING

Seniors face major concerns in today's depressed economy.

Foremost is keeping Canadian and American healthcare safe, and controlling the increasing costs of prescription medicines. In America, Medicare and Medicaid reform is essential, but seniors fear that medical services might also be cut. In Canada, seniors are organizing to save the system. Seniors United Now strives to preserve universal health care.

The key issues are reforming long term care, and enabling as many seniors as possible to receive prescription medicine discounts. Also, in Alberta, even basic health care premiums have been abolished for every one living in Alberta.

Another issue is housing. Steady drops in income combined with cost increases threaten the ability to stay in one's house or apartment. Housing can swallow much of your social security income -- whether living in rent-controlled city apartments or homes with mortgages or equity credit lines. There is also the issue of the availability of affordable housing with facilities for low-income and disabled seniors.

In Canada property taxes are steadily increasing for homeowners because of the increasing demand for public services and there are long waiting lists for seniors wanting to secure affordable housing in retirement.

A huge priority is making sure social security is available, and expanding the safety net for emergencies where both the rich and the poor share payroll and income taxes. This will minimize what Warren Buffet is noted as saying, "When it comes to the social security payroll tax, my own secretary pays more than I do."

The availability of long term care and assisted living providers for many seniors will depend on healthcare reforms to ensure care, personnel, and facilities at an affordable cost.

There is also the issue of discrimination against older workers leading to downgrading and termination of seniors. The idea that at some future time we will have a shortage of workers due to fewer births and that seniors will be able to work into old age and be prized for experience and wisdom is wishful thinking.

The fact is that the United States and Canada has become de-industrialized -- most jobs are in the service industry at minimal pay. Former manufacturers have become merely importers of foreign made products. Even administrative help is gradually reduced by automation.

Fulltime employment, once the goal of government policies, simply no longer exists.

The availability, cost, and effectiveness of social services must also be preserved. These services should include home care, nutritional services, caregiver support and respite programs, money management, financial literacy, and protective services against elder abuse and exploitation.

The government of Canada realizes the importance of financial literacy as a life skill -- especially during these times of economic challenges.

The Financial Consumer agency of Canada (FCAC) has created a task force, comprised of 13 members, who will make recommendations to the Minister of Finance on improving the coordination of financial literacy efforts.

The trend of severely diminished "nest eggs" and the disappearance of private company pensions has been a major cause of stress for seniors. They also experience psychological problems, the loss of meaningful activity, loss of self-esteem, and a lack of meaning or purpose in life. This is a form of grieving over the loss of career and meaningful work.

These problems contribute to depression, loss of energy and mobility, and can severely damage the retiree's health. Another problem arises when a healthy spouse needs to take care of a disabled spouse relative -- it takes a heavy physical and emotional toll on the caregiver.

The lack of meaningful employment of retirees represents a huge waste of talent, energy and experience that could contribute significantly to the public well-being. Does public policy affect older adults? Entitlements overall will be harder and harder to negotiate because of the current debt position of both America and Canada.

The small business option can open up entirely new experiences, new adventures, and generate a feeling of satisfaction and fulfillment -- creating an exciting and meaningful second or third stage of life. Seniors could be more creative and productive by supporting more tax credits for individuals that start up a new small business. We must abolish the idea that as seniors increase income they are penalized if receiving government benefits. Seniors deserve the right to earn small business income tax free.

With surplus income there is the opportunity to donate funds to charities in this time of lower contributions to organizations overall.

The federal and provincial governments in Canada could provide tax incentives to encourage senior entrepreneurs or encore career individuals. I suggest that government could develop and implement a TFBA (Tax Free Business Account) that could provide a minimum $10,000 - $20,000 per year small business tax deduction or equivalent tax credit for seniors.

This would empower seniors to work on desired projects and be more creative and productive throughout retirement life. Government entitlements could be relegated to a basic income source combined with productive activities such as a small business. This would provide a supplementary income tax free vehicle for active seniors.

We will need to create some small business support groups for seniors to help individuals process innovative ideas.

Peter, a former firefighter who turned 84 last May, rose up through the ranks over 35 years to retire as deputy fire chief. He has spent thousands of hours over the past five years trying to stop the clickety-clack of the railroad track. While his wife of 60 years, Janie, does a daily crossword puzzle, he has puzzled over ways to eliminate that annoying noise. What started as a hobby turned into an obsession.

Peter's silent running system would require rail manufacturers to cut the ends of length of track at a 22.5-degree angle, rather than current 90 degrees, to enable the train wheels to run along the expansion joint rather than bumping up against it. This stops the click-clacking and saves the wear and tear on the train wheels. To make it even more silent they could put lengths of old car tires under the lengths of track.

Peter says he isn't expecting to profit from his design, but he would like to see someone take it and improve on it and use that technology in places like China and India. "The idea is to pass it on and have someone do something with it," he says. "I think it's a good idea and that it should be put to use."

As I have illustrated throughout this book seniors as entrepreneurs is not necessarily about money, but the opportunity to contribute to society utilizing talents, hopes and dreams to make life better for future generations.

Chapter 8
Maturity, Wisdom, and Confidence

What makes seniors more likely to succeed in business?

Earle, L (2003) in "Background to Productive Aging" found a factor that will exert an impact upon grey entrepreneurial tendencies is the broader social context within which the individual operates.

Some societies value aging and believe that older individuals have great wisdom and experience that is an important asset; others treat the aged as largely incapable and dependent persons with little left to contribute.

If a society is supportive of independent entrepreneurs as part of what is termed "productive aging", then more individuals are likely to start or run businesses than would otherwise be the case. (Earle, 2003)

Baucus D, and Human, S.E. (1994) also provide evidence of the impact of strong networks in assisting the startup process, and suggest that such personal links can help older entrepreneurs gain both financial and marketing support.

Adequate capital to support venture formation is a key contingency in the success of entrepreneurs at any age.

SENIORPRENEUR MINDSET

C. Kumar and N. Patel, 72 years old – the inventor of the carbon dioxide laser, the holder of 38 patents, and the former head of the Physics and Engineering departments of Bell Labs – where he worked for 32 years – started his own business. Then 62, Patel sank $150,000 of his savings into launching his own company: Pramalytica.

"I guess I was trying to relive my youth," he says, "I was doing something that I had not done before."

However, Patel quickly realized that despite his vast experience he still had a lot to learn about starting his own firm. Initially, Patel's Santa Monica, California startup developed sensors that could analyze human breath for disease.

He shifted direction after realizing physicians preferred to lease rather than purchase such instruments and funding evaporated following the dot-com bust. He then began making ammonia-detection sensors for federal and state environmental protection agencies. That led to a $13 million military contract to create a device that could detect nerve gas.

Awarded an additional contract from the Defense Advanced Research Projects Agency (DARPA), the company now makes small lasers to destroy shoulder-mounted anti-aircraft missiles.

25 HOURS A DAY

Today, Pramalytica has 18 employees, and Patel says that last year's revenues hit $1 million.

He expects that to reach $8 million this year.

Patel, who will turn 72 in July, says "starting a company late in life is hard, because it takes 25 hours a day to make it successful, and there are only 24 hours in a day.

It takes intensive work to start a company and to do so at 62 is maybe not the smartest thing, but I don't regret it," he says. "It turned out well," says Patel – which is a confidence builder for seniors (50 plus). (Business Week, June 8, 2009).

These examples show that maturity, wisdom, and confidence can contribute to a successful seniorpreneur small business.

Differences in education, background, work and business experiences, or age can be overcome utilizing a laser beam kind of focus on your business idea as a successful entrepreneur.

Chapter 9
Philanthropy and Seniors Building a Legacy

Throughout this book, I have referenced Colonel Sanders as my main example of a business person utilizing his own personal circumstances to build an extraordinary business.

Sanders received the Horatio Alger Award and an honorary Doctorate from Union College of Barbourville, Kentucky. The colonel was a trailblazer at age 65 noted for his entrepreneurial activities as well as contributions to social and charity causes.

He still had enough time to build his legacy.

IS IT POSSIBLE?

It **is** possible to create and build a very productive and profitable business after 65 and at the same time have social responsibility through significant philanthropic activities.

Sanders held on to his Canadian rights in the company and established a foundation in Canada turning over his profits to charities, hospitals, the Boy Scouts, and the Salvation Army.

He also adopted 78 foreign orphans.

Today, the Colonel Harland Sanders Charitable Organization still exists in Canada.

Colonel Sanders said, "Probably I am old fashioned and don't appreciate the ways of big corporations today. The business I developed was a personal one. I knew most of the franchisees by their first names, and many of them had slept in my beds and ate breakfast at my table. We were just one big family."

In 1964, Sanders sold out to a group of investors for $2 million US. Besides the $2 million, he received a lifetime salary of $40,000 a year -- later raised to $75,000 -- to promote the business.

In most cases, you will find very rich people such as Bill Gates and Warren Buffet becoming philanthropists.

A greater emphasis has been placed on social responsibility, with the ranks of philanthropy and seniors building a legacy.

In the future, the same success could be achieved by less well-endowed senior entrepreneurs.

For example, the Running Room in Edmonton helps people maintain health through running, walking, and other forms of exercise.

The details of Colonel Sanders' registered charity can be found on www.seniorpreneur.ca.

Chapter 10
Career Transition – More Help

Are you ready to find your calling in life?

The transition from a long 30 years in the corporate life to a for-profit entrepreneurial business or a non-profit social entrepreneur is not an easy one.

The Reverend Sam Shafer, a parish priest living in Oakland, California stated three questions to help you find your calling in life.

What need in the world will ignite your passions in your heart, tap into your personal gifts and educational background, and bring new vitality to all? You might start by finding a need and pondering three not so easy to answer questions:

FINDING YOUR CALLING IN LIFE
Who am I?

Distill what you have discovered about yourself during your life and uncover the attributes that have been elusive or buried for a long time. It is also helpful if you are nobody but yourself in a world that is always trying to make you everybody else.

Fight one of the hardest battles a human being can fight -- discover a new purpose in life that will require that you to live more authentically. Do not bend to the outside forces around you.

How do I function best?

How are you wired and in what circumstances do you perform best? What natural talents and learned skills do you have to contribute? You may have knowledge of your abilities, but other gifts may be waiting to be discovered. You need to carefully assess your natural talents, favorite skills, and the fields of knowledge you have gravitated towards most of your life. What have you been praised for doing well? What experiences have you had that ignited a passion?

Why am I here?

Take as a leap of faith that you were put here for a purpose, that you have been given gifts you require to achieve your mission. What is the place that you can provide the greatest good? Finding that place may not be easy, clear, or concise because it is a work in progress.

A providential force beyond your control is always going before you and opening doors for you to walk through. It may take two to three years of shedding old ways of thinking and then you will discover your heartfelt passions.

New pathways will become clear. Remember that the journey is an integral part of the mission, and both the passionate heart and the needs of the world are constantly changing.

This time of revelation and self-discovery provides a great opportunity to probe the deep hunger within you. Take a journey to uncover the many needs in our world today and the places where you might fit in. You might find a group already addressing a need tugging at your heart and an organization in which you can be a vital participant and discover a unique solution to a problem.

This is a solution that meshes with your calling and purpose.

With the internet, everyone should be able to find a project for his or her years of wisdom, experience, and giftedness that would be of great value. Everyone offers many opportunities to connect with others who share your geographical location or passions.

We live in perilous times – a period in which the very underpinnings of our society are crumbling. Our very fabric of being is changing right in front of our eyes. Those with a goal for finding a passion for living and with eyes upon the "world's deep hunger" should build a solid foundation.

Rather than being distracted by material concerns, they are focused on caring and giving to the needs of the world around them. They are called to serve.

FEARS

Sam further advises that there are two areas in which we can expect to encounter fears and resistance of the false kind. The first is when we enter into the territory of unleashing our gifts and uncovering who we are and what we were created to be. The second area where fears can arise is when we move the direction of a calling where we can most effectively be of service to the world.

You can almost anticipate great resistance and unfounded fears when you try to enter these areas.

After all, you might just become a real tool for overcoming injustice, poverty, sickness, and the many other causes of suffering in the world around you.

TIME TO TAKE THE STAGE FOR AN ENCORE PERFORMANCE

The last impression that I want to leave you is the story of Susan Boyle. Susan participated in a singing contest in June 2009 called "Britain's Got Talent". This video can be found on YouTube.

Piers Morgan was sitting alongside fellow judges Amanda Holden and a smirking Simon Cowell. They saw this frumpy, unkempt-looking woman of a certain elderly age stride up to the stage, and one of the judges, Piers Morgan thought to himself, "Oh, for the love of God, here we go again."

Boyle was asked, "If you had some talent, why didn't you start auditioning earlier in your life?" Susan replied that she would have started her career earlier but she didn't get the chance before.

She was hoping that her current singing

audition would be good enough to advance in this particular competition.

When Susan was interviewed briefly before she was about to give her performance she couldn't remember key details about her hometown and combined with her rather unprofessional look, the audience started to laugh at her.

Isn't this a description of the situation a lot of seniors are facing today? The lack of respect leading to low self-esteem is probably why most seniors have a difficult time advancing regarding any entrepreneurial activities or encore careers.

How did Susan Boyle handle the pressure put on herself from an un-believing audience including the judges? Susan just shrugged and said, "I'm going to rock this audience." She then brought the microphone up to her mouth to sing a song titled, "I Dreamed A Dream" from the play 'Les Miserables.'

I've never seen an audience change from one moment laughing and snickering to listening to Susan's performance with total shock and amazement. The audience in unison along with the three judges right at the beginning of the performance began standing up and cheering wildly.

These cheers lasted the entire performance.

Personally, I've never been so affected by an individual performance where there was so little expectation by the audience or the judges. Just like Colonel Sanders, Susan Boyle also conquered defeat, showed up on the stage of life and both of these people performed spectacularly. By the way, Susan Boyle finished second in this competition.

Just recently Susan Boyle has made chart history after **her debut album shot straight to number one in Britain** and climbed the charts globally as well.

Boyle, who became a worldwide star after appearing on British reality television, has sold more than 410,000 copies of her album, 'I Dreamed A Dream'. A sales record for the first week of a debut album on the British charts.

This is exactly what I mean when I say:

Encore! Encore!
Seniors (50 plus) as Entrepreneurs:

Their Time Has Come.

CONCLUSION
More Empirical Research Required

After reviewing the existing knowledge on the topics of senior entrepreneurs and lifelong learning for seniors (50 plus), I conclude that more empirical research is required.

The grey entrepreneur is a highly relevant yet largely under-researched phenomenon.

Over time this segment will have a growing impact upon national and international economic performance, policy framework, academia, and business in general. As populations age, this concept will increasingly become a mainstream issue for analysis and debate.

A little is already known about this group, but much more remains to be uncovered. Greater scholarly research is therefore required to understand and encourage its activities in the 21st century.

Also, let me say that change is possible for seniors 50 and over to empower themselves and have a more creative, active and satisfying retirement life.

There are many examples of seniors like 84-year-old Peter's idea of trying to stop the clickety-clack of the railroad track (no commercial success to date); or Colonel Sander's idea of an 11 herbs and spices secret recipe chicken utilizing a pressure cooker machine (extraordinary success achieved).

A major problem found is that seniors for the most part are developing these creative or innovative ideas by themselves in isolation, rather than practicing the lifelong learning process where more help could be acquired. This would develop a team concept to get more leverage for these good business ideas.

In practice, Sanders did use the lifelong learning process literally to develop the right mixture of seasonings and the right combination of temperature, pressure and cooking time for his pressure cooker machine.

The Colonel experimented freely throughout his life before making a final business decision regarding the best available products at the time.

Also, we will need new lifelong learning centres to work with seniors to keep them motivated and to acquire more business and personal finance knowledge that can be utilized to propel any excellent ideas to the marketplace. At the same time these learning experiences will enable seniors to become more creative and productive in entrepreneurial activities.

In the end, seniors will have the opportunity to supplement retirement income and develop foundations for the social and economic benefit of society.

Finally, it is time to think of seniors as entrepreneurs or even active and productive Encore career participants, and not the traditional image of seniors as primarily being unproductive and only concerned about entitlements.

On this Encore stage, let's take a moment now to stand up and give ALL seniors a standing ovation!

Happy seniorpreneuring!

Decide not to let dreams die.

Your retirement life will be a very prosperous and healthy endeavor.

Run the last lap of your life briskly and confidently across the finish line.

Encore! Encore!

REFERENCES

1. Arkebauer, J.B. 1995 Golden Entrepreneuring; The Mature Person's Guide To A Successful Business, Mcgraw-Hill, Inc. New York

2. Weber Paul and Schaper Michael 2004, Understanding The Grey Entrepreneur, Journal Of Enterprising Culture, Vol. 12, No. 2 (June 2004) 147-164

3. Patel H. Suresh Dr. And Gray Cohn Professor, November 2006, The Grey Entrepreneurs In UK, IKD Working Paper No. 18

4. Sanders Harland Col., 1974 Life As I Have Known It Has Been "Finger Lickin' Good," Creation House, Illinois 60187

5. R. West, "An Application Of Prefrontal Cortex Function Theory Of Cognitive Aging," Psychological Bulletin 120 (1996): 272

6. About Natalie L. Denburg, Ph.D. Natalie Denburg, Ph.D., Is An Assistant Professor Of Neurology And Neuroscience At The University Of Iowa Carver College Of Medicine, Her Research Interests Involve The Neural Basis Of Decision-Making Abilities In Older Adults; Consumer, Medical And Financial Decision-

Making; Neuroepidemiology; Social And Affective Neuroscience; And Cancer Survivorship

7. About Lyndsay Harshman, B.S: Lyndsay Harshman, B.S., is a third-year medical student at the University of Iowa Career College of Medicine. She was awarded a Doris Duke clinical research fellowship for the 2008-2009 academic year

8. Older & Wiser, Richard M. Restak, M.D. Simon & Schuster, 1947

9. Footnote: The idea for "Seniors as Entrepreneurs: Their Time Has Come", came from Business Week reader Marcia McLean. McLean owns Cape Coder – a software development firm in Cape Cod, Mass.

10. Teemu Kautonen, University of Vaasa, Finland International Journal of Business Science V. Applied Management, Volume 3, Issue 3, 2008

11. Kean, R.C., Van Zandt, S. and Maupin, W. (1993) Successful Aging: The Older Entrepreneur, Journal of Women and Aging, 5(1): 25-42

12. Journal of Enterprising Culture, Vol. 12, No. 2 (June 2004) 147-164

13. Baucus, D. and Human, S.E. (1994). Second Career Entrepreneurs: A Multiple Case of Entrepreneurial Processes and Antecedent

Variables, Entrepreneurship Theory and Practice, 19(2): 41-71

14. Curran, J. and Blackburn (2001) Notes and Issues, Older People and the Enterprise Society: Age and Self-Employment Propensities, Work, Employment Society, 15(4): 889-902

15. Staudinger, U.M. (1999) Older and Wiser – Integrating Results on the Relationship Between Age and Wisdom Related Performance, International Journal of Behaviorial Development, 23(3): 641-664

16. Earle, L (2003), Background to Productive Aging

17. Thomas N. Duening (2010), Business and Entrepreneurship Director, Center for Entrepreneurship and College of Business and Administration, University of Colorado, Colorado Springs, USA. Journal of Entrepreneurship, Vol. 19, No. 1, 1-22 (2010)

18. McItay, R (2001) Women Entrepreneurs: Moving Beyond Family and Flexibility, International Journal of Entrepreneurial Behavior and Research, 7(4): 148-165

19. Peters, M. Storey, D. and Cressy, R. (1999). The Economic Impact of Aging on Entrepreneurship and SME'S, the Netherlands

EIM Small Business and Consultancy and Warwick University, Brussels.

20. Birley S. (1985) The Role of Networks in the Entrepreneurial Process, Journal of Business Venturing

21. Rotefoss and Kolvereid (2005), International Journal of Business Science and Applied Management

22. R. David Thomas (1991), Dave's Way, G.P. Putnam and Sons Publishers, P. 86-87

23 Ray Kroc with Robert Anderson (1997), Grinding it Out, The Making of McDonalds, Berkley Publishing Corporation, New York, NY

24. Mark Victor Hansen and Art Linkletter (2006), How to Make the Rest of Your Life the Best of Your Life, Nelson Books Publisher

www.ingramcontent.com/pod-product-compliance
Lightning Source LLC
Chambersburg PA
CBHW051708170526
45167CB00002B/588